This Book
Belongs To

_____

_____

_____

Age:

_____

What's a sea monster's favourite treat?

Fish and ships.

What do snowmen eat for breakfast?

Snowflakes.

Knock, knock
Who's there?
Bella.
Bella who?
Bella not working, let me in.

Why did Cinderella get kicked off the soccer team?
Because she kept on running away from the ball.

On what day do monsters eat people?
Chewsday!

Where do fish keep their money?
In the river bank.

What do you call a T-rex with a banana in each ear?
Anything you like – it can't hear you.

What vegetable is always wet?
A leek.

Where can you find fruit at the fair?
On the cherry-go-round!

What's black and white and red all over?

A penguin falling down the stairs.

Why was six afraid of seven?

Because seven ate nine.

What do traffic wardens have in their sandwiches?

Traffic jam.

What did one bee say to the other bee?

Buzz off!

Did you hear about the silly sailor?

He joined the gravy instead of the navy.
Then he sailed the seven peas, instead of the seven seas!

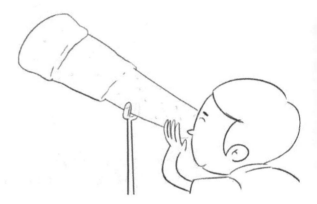

How do you find space custard?
With a jellyscope!

What kind of bow is impossible to tie?
A rainbow.

What is the largest type of ant?
A giant!

What did the snowman say to the snowoman?
What's an ice girl like you, doing in a place like this?

What do you call a dancing sheep?

A baalarina.

What pet is always smiling?

A grinnypig.

Why are fish so clever?
Because they're always in schools.

How do you catch a squirrel?
Climb up a tree and act
like a nut!

**Where can you find a
Tyrannosaurus Rex in a bikini?**
At the dino-shore.

**What do birds need when
they are sick?**
Tweetment.

What's a mouse's favourite game?

Hide and squeak!

How do horses propose?

On bended neigh!

What do frogs sing at birthday parties?

Hoppy Birthday to You!

What photos do tortoises take?

They take shellfies!

What's big, grey, and wobbly?

A jelly-phant.

What kind of fruit can you swim in?

A watermelon.

What perfume makes you smell funny?
Laughtershave!

What do snakes learn at school?
Hisstory.

What coat makes you wet?

A coat of paint.

**What do you get if you
a bear with a fridge?**

A teddy brrrrr.

What ship sails on a custard sea?

The Jelly Roger!

Who should you never play cards with in the jungle?

The cheetahs!

Why didn't the skeleton go to the ball?

Because he had no body to go with.

How do you stop a skunk from smelling?

Put a peg on its nose.

What do you get if you cross a sheep with a kangaroo?

A woolly jumper.

What does Tarzan sing at Christmas?

Jungle bells, jungle bells!

Who flies through the air in his underwear?

Peter Pants.

What monkey can float in the air?

A hot air baboon.

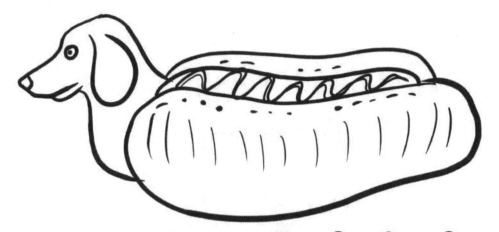

What dog smells of onions?
A hot dog.

Who stole the shower rings?
The robber ducky.

Waiter, waiter, there's a fly in my soup!

Don't worry, madam, there's no extra charge.

Waiter, there's a frog in my soup!

Don't worry, I'll tell him to hop it!

Waiter, do you have chicken legs?

No, it's just the way I walk!

What animal are you like when you take a shower?
A little bare.

What do you call a smelly fairy?
Stinkerbell!

Patient: "Doctor, doctor, I keep thinking I'm a bridge."

Doctor: "What's come over you?"

Patient: "A truck, two cars, and three buses!"

What's a cat's favourite dessert?
Mice cream.

What kind of stories do
kittens love?
Furry tales.

What do you call a cat that lives underwater?

An octopuss.

What goes up when rain comes down?

An umbrella.

Did you hear the story about
the prince who fell in love
with a cow?

It's not true, it's
just a dairy tale.

What pet makes too much noise?

A trumpet.

Where do sheep get their wool cut?

At the baabers.

What train carries a lots of toffee?

A chew, chew train.

What train carries lots of manure?

A poo, poo train.

What do you get if you sit under a cow?
A pat on the head.

What did one slug say to the other slug?
See you next slime.

What's the difference between a bird and a fly?

A bird can fly but a fly can't bird.

Did you hear about the frog whose car broke down?

He got toad away!

Knock, knock.
Who's there?
Red.
Red who?
Red any good books lately?

Knock, knock.
Who's there?
Cows go.
Cows go who?
No, cows go moo!

A Funny Poem

The spider was the head chef
The baker was a snail
They opened up a cake shop
But not one cake did they sell
But our cakes are the finest
They're made with worm and flea
Our loaves are so delicate
Spiced with wasp and bee
Why they never sold one single cake
Remains a mystery

Silly sailor Sally
Sailed the seven seas
Her sails were sown of silken threads
Her masts of Christmas trees

Why wouldn't the orange go to school?

Because he wasn't peeling well.

What's a crocodile's favourite card game?

Snap!

Where do baby apes sleep?

In apricots.

What's black and white, and goes round and round?

A penguin stuck in a washing machine.

What's wobbly and flies?
A jellycopter!

What kind of pet did Aladdin have?
A carpet!

Come Here

If Kittens were
Mittens they'd make
the Purr-fect gift

If Lions were
Irons all creases
soon would shift

If Tigers were
Taxis you wouldn't
want a lift

What do you call a rabbit with fleas?

Bugs bunny!

What do you call a witch made of sand?

A sandwich.

What did the big star say
to the little star?
You're too young to
be out at night.

Why did the cookie lose
the boxing match?
Because he was a crummy
fighter.

Why are police officers so strong?

Because they hold up traffic.

What happens when birds fall in love?

They become tweethearts!

Waiter, what's this fly doing in my soup?
It looks like he's learning to swim, sir.

Waiter, get me the manager. I can't eat this muck!
It's no use, he won't eat it either.

**What did Mr Candle say
to Mrs Candle?**

Will you go out with me tonight?

**How can you cut the ocean
in half?**

With a sea saw.

What's a cow's favourite party game?

Moosical chairs.

What type of haircut do mermaids like?

Short and pearly.

How do you start a jelly race?

Ready, set, go!

How do you start a firefly race?

Ready, set, glow!

How do you start a teddy race?

Ready, teddy, go!

What should you say to a three-headed policeman?

Hello, hello, hello.

Where do you find a dog with no legs?

Wherever you left it.

What do you call two bananas?
A pair of slippers.

Where do mice leave their boats?
At the Hickory Dickory Dock!

What colour a burp?
Burple.

What did one octopus say to the other octopus?
I want to hold your hand, hand, hand, hand, hand, hand, hand, hand!

Why did the women buy all the birds at the pet shop?

They were going cheep!

**Doctor, doctor,
I feel like a pair of
curtains!**

Pull yourself together, man.

Why do bees hum?

Because they don't know
the words.

What did the stamp say to
the envelope?

Stick with me and we'll
go places.

What did the sea say to the sand?

Nothing, it just waved.

What do you get if you cross a jelly with a skunk?

Smelly jelly!

Knock, knock.
Who's there?
Orange.
Orange who?
Orange you glad to see me?

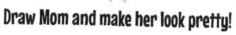

Draw Mom and make her look pretty!

Thanks Mom!

Thank you for purchasing
my book. If you enjoyed it,
please give it a review!

The Joy of the Lord
Is My Strength!

JOKES AND POEMS BY
CINDY MERRYLOVE
MR KRISPELL
CHARLOTTE COLLINGWOOD

Printed in the United States of America

First Printing, 2018

Contact: Sniffitysnoo302@gmail.com

An awesome joke book
for older children!

THE BEST JOKE BOOK FOR KIDS

A children's Joke Book
The Whole Family Will Love!

By Cindy Merrylove